THIS BOOK IS BELONGS TO:

Made in the USA
Monee, IL
08 June 2022

97592801R00068